Published in 2014 by The Rosen Publishing Group, Inc.
29 East 21st Street, New York, NY 10010

Photo Credits: **KEY** tl=top left; tr=top right; cl=center left; c=center; cr=center right; bl=bottom left; bc=bottom center; br=bottom right; bg=background

CBT = Corbis; DSCD = Digital Stock; GI = Getty Images; iS = istockphoto.com; N = NASA; SH = Shutterstock

Cover SH **6**bl CBT; cl iS; bg N; bc, c SH; **6–7**bg N; **8**bl, br, cl, cr DSCD; **9**bl, cl, tl DSCD; **16**bl CBT; **23**br CBT; **25**cl iS; **26–27**cl GI; **27**tr CBT; **29**bl iS; **32**bg N

All illustrations copyright Weldon Owen Pty Ltd

WELDON OWEN PTY LTD
Managing Director: Kay Scarlett
Creative Director: Sue Burk
Publisher: Helen Bateman
Senior Vice President, International Sales: Stuart Laurence
Vice President Sales North America: Ellen Towell
Administration Manager, International Sales: Kristine Ravn

Publisher Cataloging Data

McFadzean, Lesley.
Earthquakes: on shaky ground / by Lesley McFadzean.
p. cm. — (Discovery education: earth and space science)
Includes index.
ISBN 978-1-4777-6182-3 (library binding) — ISBN 978-1-4777-6184-7 (pbk.) —
ISBN 978-1-4777-6185-4 (6-pack)
1. Earthquakes — Juvenile literature. I. McFadzean, Lesley. II. Title. 54/4 37/3 06/14
QE521.3 M37 2014
363.34—d23

Manufactured in the United States of America

CPSIA Compliance Information: Batch #W14PK2: For Further Information contact Rosen Publishing, New York, New York at 1-800-237-9932

EARTH AND SPACE SCIENCE

EARTHQUAKES
ON SHAKY GROUND

Lesley McFadzean

Contents

Inside Earth

Planet Earth is not simply a solid ball of rock. Of Earth's four layers, only the inner core is solid. The outer core is so hot that it is liquid. The mantle is mostly solid rock mixed with rocks that have melted to form a thick liquid called magma. The crust is solid rock, but made up of slabs, or plates, with cracks or faults between them. Many of Earth's dramatic landforms, from mountains to deep rift valleys, were created by movements beneath Earth's crust.

Earth's layers

The solid rocks on Earth's crust shift and move on top of the hot rocks and magma of the mantle. The energy comes from an inner core as hot as the surface of the Sun.

Fault lines
A long and narrow crack, or fault, in Earth's crust runs through Thingvellir, Iceland.

Lift and tilt
Movement from beneath Earth's crust can lift and tilt rocks.

Folds in rocks
Compression, from two different directions, causes rock layers to bend or fold.

Geyser
Magma-heated water deep underground erupts to the surface as a geyser.

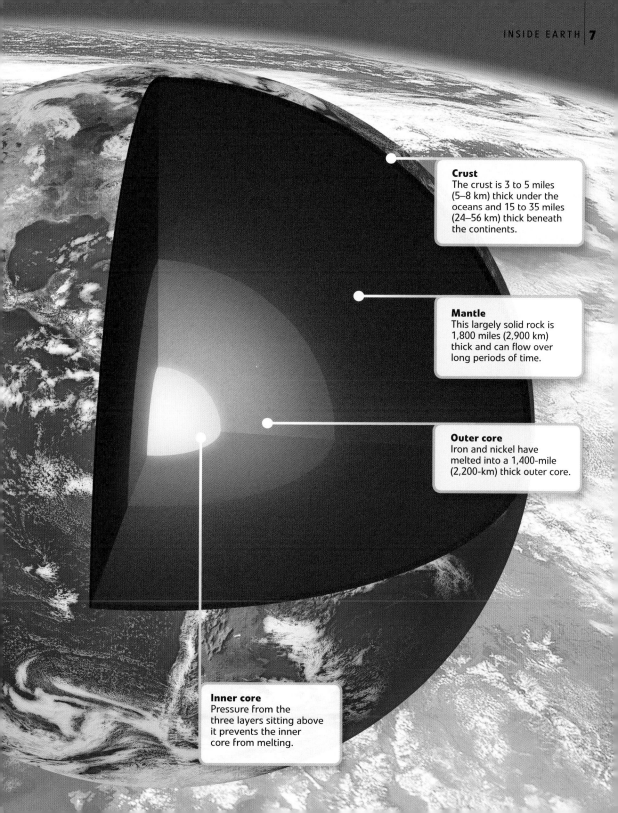

Crust
The crust is 3 to 5 miles (5–8 km) thick under the oceans and 15 to 35 miles (24–56 km) thick beneath the continents.

Mantle
This largely solid rock is 1,800 miles (2,900 km) thick and can flow over long periods of time.

Outer core
Iron and nickel have melted into a 1,400-mile (2,200-km) thick outer core.

Inner core
Pressure from the three layers sitting above it prevents the inner core from melting.

Tectonic Plates

Earth's crust and the upper part of the mantle, called the lithosphere, are made up of dozens of tectonic plates. These plates are rigid slabs around 60 miles (100 km) thick. They "float" on the lower part of the mantle—the molten rock of the asthenosphere—and move constantly. Seven of these tectonic plates are very large. It is at the boundaries of these plates that most of Earth's earthquakes and volcanoes occur.

Fact or Fiction?

Tectonic plates move at the same rate at which fingernails grow. This is fact! Plates move and nails grow around 2 inches (5 cm) in one year.

Pacific plate
This forms the ocean floor for most of the Pacific Ocean. Underwater mountains, volcanic islands, and deep trenches, such as Challenger Deep (the world's deepest point), were created by Pacific plate movements.

Eurasian plate
This plate has boundaries with many other plates. The world's highest mountain range, the Himalayas, as well as the Alps, were created by movements of the Eurasian plate.

African plate
Half of this plate is under the continent of Africa. The other, heavier half is under the Indian, Atlantic, and Southern oceans. Africa's Great Rift Valley and the mid-Atlantic ridge are features of the African plate.

Indo-Australian plate
Ocean ridges are features on the western and southern areas of this plate. To the north and east, the boundaries are part of the Pacific Ring of Fire, where 75 percent of the world's volcanoes are located.

Antarctic plate

The Antarctic plate has boundaries with six other tectonic plates, including the South American, African, Pacific, and Indo-Australian plates. Movements at these boundaries are nearly all divergent, that is, away from, rather than toward, each other.

North American plate

Lying under North America and part of the Atlantic Ocean, this plate contains some of Earth's oldest rocks. Collisions with the Pacific plate created the mountain ranges along the west coast of North America.

South American plate

The smallest of the seven plates lies partly under the continent of South America and partly under the Atlantic Ocean. Movements in the South American plate created the Andes mountains.

Plate boundaries

The part of Earth's crust where two plates meet is called a plate boundary. Movement in the hot mantle causes the plates to move in different directions.

Sliding past
Two plates that slide in opposite directions past each other create a transform fault boundary.

Moving apart
A divergent boundary, where two plates move away from each other, thins or creates a gap in Earth's crust.

Collision
A convergent boundary is one where two plates move toward or collide with each other.

Fault Lines

Just like bones, rocks can fracture under extreme pressure. These fractures, or fault lines, appear in Earth's crust where two or more tectonic plates meet. There are three major types of faults: normal, reverse, and strike-slip faults. The type of fault depends on whether the plate boundary is divergent, convergent, or transform. Whatever the type of fault, when rocks on each side of the fault line grind against each other, an earthquake can occur.

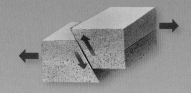

Normal fault
This occurs at divergent plate boundaries. As the plates pull apart, one side slips downward.

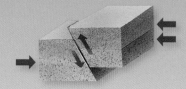

Reverse fault
This occurs at convergent plate boundaries. As the plates push into each other, one side of the fault is pushed upward.

STRIKE-SLIP FAULT

The boundary between the North American and Pacific plates is a transform fault boundary. The Pacific plate is moving northwest and the North American plate is moving southeast in this strike-slip fault.

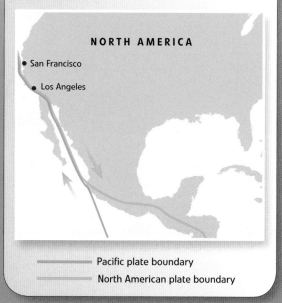

NORTH AMERICA

• San Francisco

• Los Angeles

——— Pacific plate boundary

——— North American plate boundary

That's Amazing!
The San Andreas Fault zone has many smaller faults branching off it. These cause thousands of earthquakes in California every year, many not large enough to be noticed.

Fault lines around the world
A map of the world's fault lines also indicates volcanic and earthquake activity throughout the world. Tremors do travel, however, so they can affect parts of the world hundreds of miles (km) from a fault line.

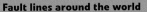

EURASIAN PLATE

NORTH AMERICAN PLATE

PACIFIC PLATE

PACIFIC PLATE

AFRICAN PLATE

SOUTH AMERICAN PLATE

SOMALI PLATE

INDO-AUSTRALIAN PLATE

NAZCA PLATE

ANTARCTIC PLATE

KEY

—— Major transform fault
‡ Minor transform fault
—— Plate boundary

San Andreas Fault zone

The North American and Pacific plates have moved 350 miles (565 km) in opposite directions over the past 150 million years. Solid rock has cracked to form the 800-mile (1,290-km) long San Andreas Fault zone, parts of which are 10 miles (16 km) deep. The same movements that created this strike-slip fault have pushed up mountain ranges along the west coast of the US or stretched apart to form large valleys.

Earthquake

As the two sides of fractured rock at a fault line strain against each other, stress builds up. When one side or the other eventually gives way, there is a jolt. Vibrations pass through the rock as the built-up stress or energy is released as an earthquake. Every year there are half a million earthquakes around the world. Only 100,000 of these are strong enough to be felt, and only 100 are strong enough to cause damage.

Did You Know?

Apollo astronauts set up seismographs on the Moon to measure seismic activity. "Moonquakes" do occur but are smaller and less frequent than earthquakes on Earth.

HOW CAN THEY TELL?

For centuries, people have believed that animals can sense when an earthquake is about to happen because they start acting strangely. However, it is still unclear how reliable this belief is.

Odd animal behavior may indicate an oncoming earthquake.

Electricity
Live power lines can electrocute. When power is cut, often to large areas, normal life becomes difficult.

Ongoing damage

When a major earthquake occurs, some damage is immediately obvious. Buildings collapse, bridges fall, and chasms may open up in roads. It is often the less obvious damage, however, that causes problems in the days and weeks to come. Aftershocks that follow an earthquake can cause damaged buildings to collapse, and everyday life becomes difficult in a city that has been devastated by an earthquake.

Pipelines
Broken water pipes leak much-needed fresh water. Leaking gas pipes can be lethal. Smashed drainage pipes can cause disease.

Roads
Split, cracked, and holed roads make it almost impossible to get emergency supplies into areas affected by an earthquake.

Measuring Earthquakes

Two measures of earthquake intensity, or magnitude, are in use today. The modified Mercalli scale measures the effects of an earthquake on the environment, as reported by observers. No instruments are required since the scale relies on eyewitness reports. The Richter scale uses a seismograph to take physical measurements of earthquake intensity. This scale is more objective than the modified Mercalli scale.

Ancient seismometer
Ancient Chinese seismometers had a firm base and a weighted pendulum that swung free. During a tremor, the pendulum swayed, and a bronze ball dropped from a dragon's mouth into a toad's mouth. Seismographs these days are built on similar principles, but the weighted pendulum uses a pen to record the shock waves on a rotating drum of paper.

Modified Mercalli scale

Mercalli's original 1902 scale had only 10 (X) degrees. In 1931, two degrees were added, making a total of 12 (XII). This modified Mercalli scale is used today.

I People do not feel any Earth movements at all.

II A few people indoors, who are lying still or on a top floor, feel movement.

III Many people indoors feel movement; hanging objects swing backward and forward.

IV Most people indoors feel movement; windows rattle; parked cars rock.

V Nearly everyone feels movement; people wake; dishes break; trees shake.

VI Everyone feels movement; walking is hard; objects fall; plaster cracks.

VII It is difficult to stand; cars shake; loose bricks fall; buildings are slightly damaged.

VIII Drivers cannot steer; houses shift on foundations; chimneys fall; hillsides crack.

IX Major damage occurs to buildings; underground pipes break; the ground cracks.

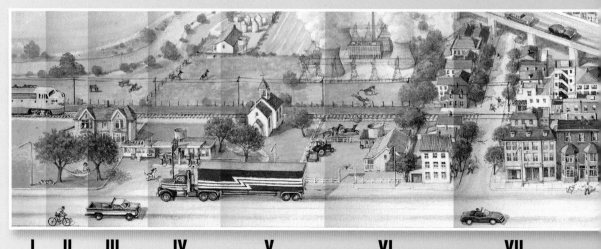

I   II   III   IV   V   VI   VII

RICHTER SCALE

The Richter scale measures the size, or amplitude, of the largest horizontal seismic motion recorded. For each number on the Richter scale, the recorded amplitude goes up by a factor of 10. A magnitude 2 earthquake therefore has 10 times the amplitude of a magnitude 1 earthquake.

Magnitude 1–2
Detected only by seismographs near the epicenter.

Magnitude 2–3
Might be felt by some people near the epicenter.

Magnitude 3–4
People feel slight tremors; lights swing; there is little damage.

Magnitude 4–5
Strong tremors are felt; windows crack; buildings are damaged.

Magnitude 5–6
Very strong tremors are felt; people start to panic; walls crack.

Magnitude 6–7
This is a severe earthquake; chimneys fall; some buildings collapse.

Magnitude 7–8
The ground cracks; more buildings collapse; widespread panic.

Magnitude 8–9
Massive destruction; bridges collapse; train tracks and roads buckle.

X Building foundations are destroyed; landslides occur; bridges fall; train tracks bend.

XI Buildings collapse; bridges and pipelines are destroyed; large cracks form in ground.

XII Near total destruction; heavy objects are thrown in air; ground moves in waves.

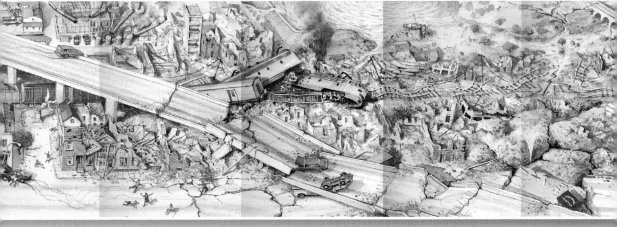

VIII   IX   X   XI   XII

Earthquake Rescue

The priority after an earthquake is to locate buried survivors who will die if they are not found quickly. However, many of the collapsed buildings are unstable and may collapse further. Fire, from ruptured gas pipes, often follows an earthquake. Aftershocks also make rescue efforts more difficult. Specially trained teams, which have knowledge of earthquakes and their aftermath, are the best hope for buried survivors.

That's Amazing!

After the 2010 Haiti earthquake, 43 international search and rescue teams, 1,750 trained rescuers, and 161 rescue dogs were flown into the area from all around the world.

Listening in
Sensitive microphones can detect the slightest sounds under the rubble. These can pinpoint a survivor's location.

RESCUE DOGS

Dogs have a much better sense of smell than humans. They are used in search and rescue operations after earthquakes and other natural disasters. The dogs require special training in a situation that is similar to the destruction of an earthquake.

This dog is searching for survivors of an earthquake.

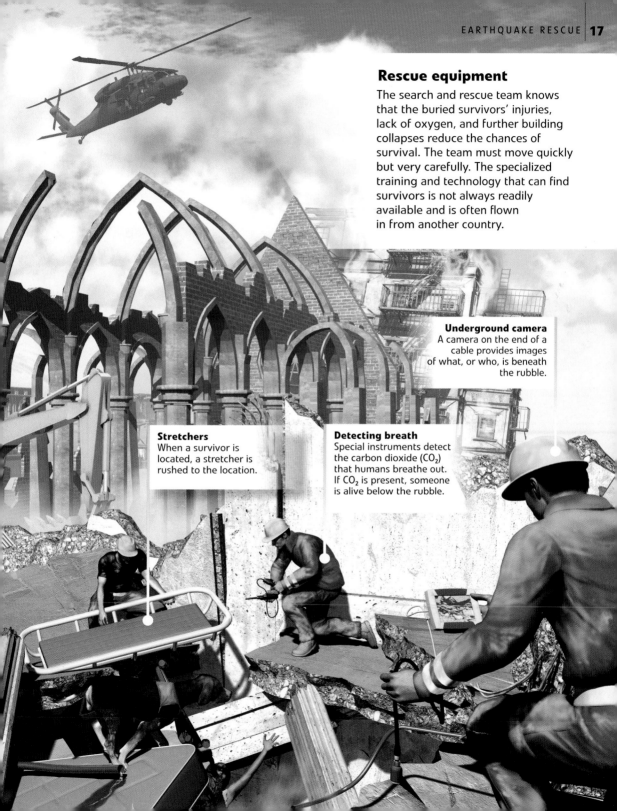

Rescue equipment

The search and rescue team knows that the buried survivors' injuries, lack of oxygen, and further building collapses reduce the chances of survival. The team must move quickly but very carefully. The specialized training and technology that can find survivors is not always readily available and is often flown in from another country.

Underground camera
A camera on the end of a cable provides images of what, or who, is beneath the rubble.

Stretchers
When a survivor is located, a stretcher is rushed to the location.

Detecting breath
Special instruments detect the carbon dioxide (CO_2) that humans breathe out. If CO_2 is present, someone is alive below the rubble.

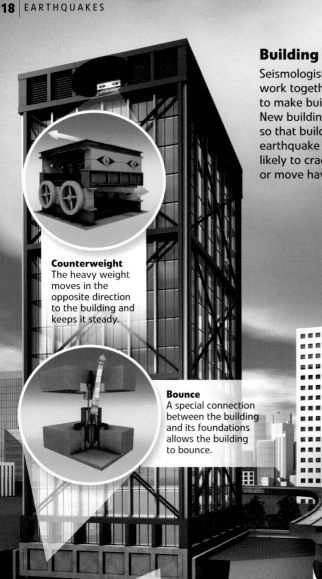

Building design

Seismologists, architects, and engineers now work together on new construction methods to make buildings more earthquake resistant. New building techniques have been developed so that buildings absorb some of the energy of earthquake tremors. Rigid buildings are more likely to crack and collapse. Those that sway or move have more chance of staying up.

Counterweight
The heavy weight moves in the opposite direction to the building and keeps it steady.

Strong pillars
Strong, steel-enmeshed concrete pillars can resist the shocks of an earthquake.

Bounce
A special connection between the building and its foundations allows the building to bounce.

Slider
A slider in the foundations allows the building to move horizontally, rather than strain and crack.

Tunnel
Gas, electricity, water, and phone lines are protected in a reinforced tunnel beneath the building.

BUILT TO STAND

Many Buddhist pagodas in Japan have survived hundreds of earthquakes and still stand, 1,000 years after they were built. This is because, when an earthquake hits, the central pillar absorbs much of the shock. The five stories, which are totally separate from each other, bend and weave on the central pillar, similar to branches on a tree trunk.

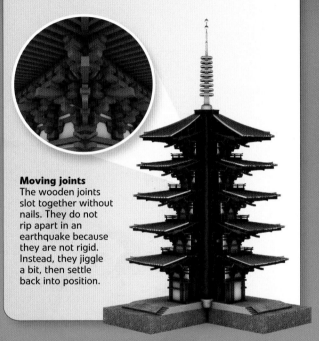

Moving joints
The wooden joints slot together without nails. They do not rip apart in an earthquake because they are not rigid. Instead, they jiggle a bit, then settle back into position.

How to Prepare

Earthquake scientists, called seismologists, know where earthquakes are most likely to occur. They can measure earthquakes when they do occur, but they cannot yet predict exactly when and where an earthquake will occur. Those who live in areas affected by earthquakes must prepare in advance, just in case. New building techniques and careful selection of the sites for private and public buildings can minimize the damage and the number of buildings that collapse in an earthquake. This, in turn, saves lives.

Home safety

For people living in an earthquake zone, preparing their homes for the next big earthquake is vital. Many children learn at school what they should and should not do in an earthquake.

Fix furniture in place
Furniture fixed to a wall will not fall on top of anyone during an earthquake.

Turn off gas
Leaking gas from broken pipes can explode or cause suffocation, so gas is turned off.

Take cover
Sturdy furniture, away from windows, provides protection from falling masonry.

Famous Earthquakes

Some earthquakes are remembered longer than others. The most famous in history are not necessarily the strongest, as measured on the Richter scale. Often, what is triggered by the earthquake makes it memorable. A tsunami or raging fire, which occurs after the ground has stopped shaking, often causes more death and destruction than the earthquake itself. Sometimes a single earthquake, or its aftermath, affects a large number of countries around the world, so it is difficult to forget.

Epicenter
This was in the Atlantic Ocean, 120 miles (190 km) offshore from Lisbon.

Lisbon, Portugal
November 1755

The Great Lisbon Earthquake, which lasted less than 10 minutes, affected all of Europe. A fire and a tsunami followed and, between them, caused the deaths of more than 60,000 people. Before 1755, earthquakes were seen as acts of God, but the devastation and death caused by the Lisbon earthquake marked the start of earthquake science.

Tsunami deaths
Thousands who survived the earthquake were drowned by the giant tsunami that followed, half an hour later.

Home damage
The earthquake struck at 5:00 a.m. when most people were at home. Many wooden houses survived the earthquake better than brick-built homes.

Destructive fire
Coal and wood-burning stoves, tipped over by the earthquake, were largely responsible for the fire that followed. The wooden homes that remained standing after the earthquake provided fuel for the devastating fire.

San Francisco
April 1906

The 1906 San Francisco earthquake lasted for less than one minute but caused massive destruction of buildings, many of which were built on unstable land. This earthquake ranks as one of the worst natural disasters in US history. Although the official death toll was 478, it is estimated that up to 6,000 died in the earthquake or the fire that followed it.

Ripple effect
Shock waves were felt all along the San Andreas Fault zone.

That's Amazing!
The "ham and eggs" fire, one of many after the 1906 San Francisco earthquake, started in a stove with an earthquake-damaged chimney. It destroyed a 30-block area of the city.

Hebgen Lake, Montana
August 1959

The largest earthquake in Montana measured 7.5 on the Richter scale and was caused by movements on a number of fault lines at the same time. Because the earthquake struck in an underpopulated rural area, the death toll was low. However, the landscape around Hebgen Lake was permanently altered: a massive landslide dammed the Madison River to create a new lake; steam vents invaded some cracks in Earth's crust to produce new geysers; and new, steep rock faces were exposed.

Hebgen Lake
This remote lake sits on the Madison River near the state border of Montana and Wyoming.

> *The Hebgen Lake earthquake was felt in nine western US states and three Canadian provinces.*

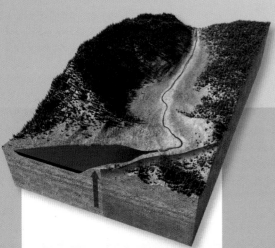

First jolt
The earthquake jolted rock layers upward by as much as 20 feet (6 m) along the existing faults northeast of Hebgen Lake. Rock layers on one side of the fault subsided up to 10 feet (3 m).

Changed landscape

The earthquake lasted less than 45 seconds but was so powerful that it activated movement along several large faults north of the lake, and many small faults south of it. Some areas were jolted upward and others dropped, or subsided.

Immediate effects
The seismic shocks loosened the south face of the steep Madison Canyon, starting a landslide that blocked the gorge. The bedrock beneath the lake warped, causing the water in the lake to slosh and surge in what is called a seiche.

Rock Creek campsite

At 6:37 a.m., when the earthquake struck, most of the campers at the Rock Creek public campsite on the Madison River were sound asleep. The jolt of the earthquake started a huge landslide, or avalanche, of rocks and soil on the steep wall of Madison River Canyon. The landslide buried the campsite, and 28 campers died.

New landscape

Up to 1,170 million cubic feet (33 million m³) of rocks, soil, and trees from the landslide formed a barrier on the river. Over the next few weeks, a new 175-foot (53-m) deep lake formed behind the barrier. The lake was named Quake, or Earthquake, Lake.

Fault scarps

Seen here as the light brown band, new fault scarps, or cliff lines, appeared in the earthquake area as the rock strata on one side of the fault slipped down.

Kobe, Japan
January 1995

The Kobe earthquake measured 6.9–7.3 on the Richter scale and was over in 20 seconds, leaving chaos in its wake. Although other parts of Japan are prepared for earthquakes, the port of Kobe was not considered to be a high-risk city. Buildings and bridges were not built to be earthquake-resistant, so damage was extensive. More than 6,000 people died, 300,000 lost their homes, and the damage bill was one of the highest in history.

Epicenter
The Kobe earthquake's epicenter was off Awaji Island, 12 miles (20 km) from the city.

Expressway damage

The 20-second earthquake was enough for 10 separate spans on the raised Hanshin Expressway to collapse. The reinforced concrete columns that elevated the expressway were unable to cope with the shock waves.

Before
Each of the concrete columns supported the weight above it and was held together with vertical steel rods.

Cracking
Strong horizontal movement cracked the concrete and broke the bond between the concrete and steel.

Collapse
As the concrete crumbled, the full weight was transferred to the steel rods, which buckled.

Epicenter
This earthquake's epicenter was 155 miles (250 km) southeast of Banda Aceh, Indonesia.

Sumatra-Andaman, Indian Ocean
December 2004

One of the world's worst natural disasters in centuries was triggered by the Sumatra–Andaman earthquake, which measured 9.1 on the Richter scale, on December 26, 2004. Under the Indian Ocean, off Indonesia, one tectonic plate slid beneath another plate, causing a megathrust earthquake. It took between 15 minutes and seven hours for devastating tsunamis to hit 11 countries, killing more than 225,000 people.

Banda Aceh
The only large city that was damaged extensively by the earthquake itself was Banda Aceh, in Indonesia. The earthquake lasted for nearly five minutes, much longer than most earthquakes. Although traditional wood-framed one- or two-story homes survived the earthquake, almost all buildings over three stories were destroyed.

Tsunami formation

An earthquake under the ocean jolts the sea bed upward. An enormous amount of water is displaced and begins to move outward from the epicenter.

All is quiet
Out at sea, the tsunami builds up and water travels at the speed of a jetliner.

Water disappears
Coastal water, located in bays and beaches, disappears as it is drawn into the tsunami.

Tsunami hits
As the tsunami hits the shore, the top of the wave can reach a height of 100 feet (30 m).

Haiti
January 2010

Haiti's earthquake, which measured 7.0 on the Richter scale, occurred at a strike-slip fault on the boundary of the North American and Caribbean plates. There were 59 aftershocks with magnitudes between 4.5 and 6.0.

The results were devastating for the capital, Port-au-Prince, as well as southern Haiti. More than half a million people were killed or injured.

Port–au–Prince
The earthquake struck 15 miles (25 km) southwest of Haiti's capital, Port-au-Prince.

Makeshift camps

Port-au-Prince is a densely populated city. The earthquake destroyed or damaged almost 300,000 homes and displaced more than a million people. Makeshift camps were set up in parks and other open grounds.

Did You Know?

The Haitian earthquake (7.0 on the Richter scale) released a hundredth of the seismic energy of the Sumatra–Andaman earthquake (9.1 on the Richter scale).

Devastation

The earthquake's actual center, or hypocenter, was only 6 miles (10 km) beneath Earth's crust, so little of the earthquake's energy was absorbed before it hit Haiti. As a result, damage and destruction were severe.

10 ANDREANOF ISLANDS, ALASKA

DATE: March 9, 1957

RICHTER SCALE: 8.6

MERCALLI SCALE: XII

DEATHS: None

2 PRINCE WILLIAM SOUND, ALASKA

DATE: March 28, 1964

RICHTER SCALE: 9.2

MERCALLI SCALE: XII

DEATHS: 130

NORTH AMERICA

6 OFFSHORE ECUADOR–COLOMBIA

DATE: January 31, 1906

RICHTER SCALE: 8.8

MERCALLI SCALE: XII

DEATHS: Up to 1,500

7 RAT ISLANDS, ALASKA

DATE: February 4, 1965

RICHTER SCALE: 8.7

MERCALLI SCALE: XII

DEATHS: None

World's Worst Earthquakes

SOUTH AMERICA

5 OFFSHORE MAULE, CHILE

DATE: February 27, 2010

RICHTER SCALE: 8.8

MERCALLI SCALE: XII

DEATHS: More than 700

Many extremely large earthquakes are known to have occurred before 1900. These include a massive earthquake in China in 1556, which killed more than 830,000 people, and a twelfth-century earthquake in Syria, which killed 230,000. However, it is only since the early twentieth century that magnitudes could be accurately measured. This map shows the date, location, and death toll of the 10 strongest earthquakes, with magnitudes higher than 8.5 on the Richter scale, since 1900.

1 VALDIVIA, CHILE

DATE: May 22, 1960

RICHTER SCALE: 9.5

MERCALLI SCALE: XII

DEATHS: 1,655

About 500,000 tremors occur every year. Most occur in the ocean crust or non-populated areas.

4 KAMCHATKA PENINSULA, RUSSIA

DATE: November 4, 1952

RICHTER SCALE: 9.0

MERCALLI SCALE: XII

DEATHS: None reported

9 ASSAM–TIBET

DATE: August 15, 1950

RICHTER SCALE: 8.6

MERCALLI SCALE: XII

DEATHS: At least 780

ASIA

EUROPE

3 SUMATRA–ANDAMAN, INDIAN OCEAN

DATE: December 26, 2004

RICHTER SCALE: 9.1

MERCALLI SCALE: XII

DEATHS: 228,000

AFRICA

TOP TEN

1 Valdivia, Chile

2 Prince William Sound, Alaska

3 Sumatra–Andaman, Indian Ocean

4 Kamchatka Peninsula, Russia

5 Offshore Maule, Chile

6 Offshore Ecuador–Colombia

7 Rat Islands, Alaska

8 Northern Sumatra, Indonesia

9 Assam–Tibet

10 Andreanof Islands, Alaska

AUSTRALIA

8 NORTHERN SUMATRA, INDONESIA

DATE: March 28, 2005

RICHTER SCALE: 8.6

MERCALLI SCALE: XII

DEATHS: 1,300

Glossary

aftershock (AF-tur-shok)
A tremor, or series of tremors, that follows the main shock of an earthquake, as two tectonic plates continue to move and adjust to their new positions. Aftershocks are smaller in magnitude than the main earthquake but can continue for many weeks, months, or even years.

amplitude
(AM-pluh-tood)
The height of the shock waves of an earthquake as recorded on a seismograph.

asthenosphere
(as-THEE-nu-sfeer)
The lower part of Earth's upper mantle, beneath the lithosphere. It is made up of soft rock.

convergent boundary
(kun-VUR-junt BOWN-duh-ree)
The boundary between two tectonic plates that are moving toward each other.

core (KOR)
The deepest of planet Earth's four layers, and the center of Earth. It is made up of a solid inner part and a hot, liquid outer part.

crust (KRUST)
The uppermost or outer layer of planet Earth. It varies in thickness and is up to nine times thicker beneath the continents than it is beneath the oceans.

divergent boundary
(duh-VUR-junt BOWN-duh-ree)
The meeting point of two tectonic plates moving very slowly away from each other.

epicenter (EH-pih-sen-tur)
The point on Earth's surface directly above the focus, or hypocenter, of an earthquake deep beneath the crust.

fault (FAWLT)
A fracture in rocks where the rock on either side of the fracture is moving.

geyser (GY-zur)
A spring that throws up jets of water and steam, heated by hot rock deep in Earth's crust.

hypocenter
(HY-puh-sen-tur)
The place deep below Earth's crust, where the energy of an earthquake is first released.

landform (LAND-form)
Any natural formation of rock and soil on Earth's surface, including large mountain ranges, plateaus, and plains, as well as smaller hills and valleys.

lithosphere
(LIH-thuh-sfeer)
The solid layer of rock in Earth's crust and the upper part of the mantle.

magma (MAG-muh)
Molten (melted) or partly molten rock beneath Earth's surface. When magma erupts in a volcano and reaches Earth's surface, it is called lava.

magnitude
(MAG-nih-tood)
The intensity of an earthquake measured and represented by a number on the Richter or modified Mercalli scale.

mantle (MAN-tul)
The layer in planet Earth that lies between the crust and the core, and contains hot, solid rock and molten rock, or magma.

megathrust

(MEH-guh-thrust)
A very severe earthquake that occurs when one tectonic plate is forced under another and huge stress builds up because the plates are locked together.

Mercalli scale

(mer-KA-lee SKAYL)
A scale, invented by Guiseppe Mercalli in the late nineteenth century, used to measure the intensity of earthquakes. The modified Mercalli scale, used today, measures the severity of an earthquake from descriptions of the shaking by those who were there.

normal fault

(NOR-mul FAWLT)
A fault where two rock walls are pulling away from each other and one wall, called the hanging wall, moves downward relative to the other wall, called the footwall.

reverse fault

(rih-VERS FAWLT)
A fault where two rock walls are pushing against each other and one wall, called the hanging wall, moves upward relative to the other wall, called the footwall.

Richter scale

(RIK-tur SKAYL)
A scale, developed by Charles Richter in 1935, that measures the magnitude of an earthquake, using a seismograph, and allocates a number from 1 to 10 to rank its severity.

scarp (SKARP)

A cliff or escarpment along the edge of a plateau, created by fault movement.

seiche (SAYCH)

Waves in the water of a lake that do not move forward, just up and down. Called standing waves, they can be started by a number of things, including earthquakes. The movement may continue after the earthquake is over.

seismic (SYZ-mik)

Anything related to or caused by an earthquake.

seismograph

(SYZ-muh-graf)
An instrument that detects, records, and measures the intensity of an earthquake.

seismologist

(syz-MAH-luh-jist)
A scientist who studies and records earthquakes and volcanoes.

strike–slip fault

(STRYK SLIP FAWLT)
A fault where two rock walls slide or grind horizontally (sideways) to the left or right in relation to each other.

tectonic plates

(tek-TAH-nik PLAYTS)
Large, thick plates in Earth's crust that move horizontally (sideways) or vertically (up and down) on the fluid, lower part of the upper mantle.

transform fault boundary

(TRANTS-form FAWLT BOWN-duh-ree)
A boundary between tectonic plates where the plates slide or glide horizontally (sideways) against each other.

tsunami (soo-NAH-mee)

A long and high ocean wave, created by undersea movements or an earthquake, that is extremely destructive when it reaches the shore.

Index

Websites

Due to the changing nature of Internet links, PowerKids Press has developed an online list of websites related to the subject of this book. This site is updated regularly. Please use this link to access the list:

www.powerkidslinks.com/disc/quakes/